# THE
## Lord's
## Prayer

# THE
# *Lord's*
# *Prayer*

PEACE AND SELF-ACCEPTANCE FOR
THOSE IN RECOVERY

## Isabel Anders

*A division of*
**THOMAS NELSON PUBLISHERS**
Nashville

Published in Nashville, Tennessee, by Oliver-Nelson Books, a division of Thomas Nelson, Inc., Publishers, and distributed in Canada by Lawson Falle, Ltd., Cambridge, Ontario.

Unless otherwise noted, the Bible version used in this publication is THE NEW KING JAMES VERSION. Copyright © 1979, 1980, 1982, Thomas Nelson, Inc., Publishers.

Verses marked TLB are taken from *The Living Bible*, copyright 1971 by Tyndale House Publishers, Wheaton, IL. Used by permission.

Scripture quotations marked NIV are taken from the HOLY BIBLE: NEW INTERNATIONAL VERSION. Copyright © 1973, 1978, 1984 by the International Bible Society. Used by permission of Zondervan Bible Publishers.

Excerpt from *His Thoughts Said . . . His Father Said* by Amy Carmichael, copyright 1941 Dohnavur Fellowship (Ft. Washington, PA: Christian Literature Crusade). Used by permission.

Printed in the United States.

**Library of Congress Cataloging-in-Publication Data**

Anders, Isabel, 1946–
    The Lord's prayer : peace and self-acceptance for those in recovery / Isabel Anders.
       p.    cm.
    Includes bibliographical references.
    ISBN 0-8407-9156-9
    1. Lord's prayer—Meditations.   2. Alcoholics—Religious life.
3. Twelve-step programs—Religious aspects—Christianity.
I. Title.
BV230.A63   1991
242'.722—dc20                   91-28834
                                     CIP

*For*

*Ruth Harms Calkin*


*I would like to express appreciation to four people*

*who especially made this book possible:*

*Jane Jordan Browne, my agent;*

*Victor Oliver, my publisher;*

*and LaVonne Neff and Aida Rawlins*

*for their friendship and encouragement.*

# CONTENTS

# THE Lord's Prayer

*I* WANT those already wise to become the wiser . . . by exploring the depths of meaning in these nuggets of truth.
—Proverbs 1:5–6 TLB

*T*ODAY is only a small manageable segment of time in which our difficulties need not overwhelm us. This lifts from our hearts and minds the heavy weight of both past and future.
—*One Day at a Time in Al-Anon*

# How This Book Is Organized

THE beloved phrases of the Lord's Prayer are here presented, paired with slogans from Al-Anon, to help the reader reflect on various aspects of true prayer as it pertains to recovery and wholeness.

Each chapter will use examples and anecdotes from life and literature to show how prayer touches all areas of our lives and attitudes when we turn our hearts over to God and seek serenity in everyday living.

True prayer is, after all, aligning ourselves with God's will and seeking to conform ourselves daily, in simple ways, to that will. It involves acceptance as well as action, discernment as well as patience with others.

When seen in the context of the Christian life and the life of recovery, the slogans covered here are far from simplistic, simple though they may sound. What is needed to make them come alive is their application to our own individual lives, day by day. Only we can add the ingredient of *actual practice,* in patience and stumbling, learning and regrouping, returning to Scripture for new insight, and opening ourselves to what God will show us of *how to live.*

Here are some very special "nuggets of truth," found in the world's most famous prayer and in our tradition of recovery, which capsulize wisdom and make it accessible for each of us, day by day. May they help us to become wiser and more compassionate in our life together in Christ.

—Isabel Anders
*Winchester, Tennessee*

# Introduction

FOR where two or three are gathered together in My name, I am there in the midst of them.

—Matthew 18:20

UNDERSTANDING is a wellspring of life to [one] who has it.

—Proverbs 16:22

The Lord's Prayer, perhaps the most well-known prayer, was called by early Christian apologist Tertullian "the summary of the whole Gospel." The prayer is found in its longer form in the gospel of Matthew, chapter 6, in the midst of Jesus' Sermon on the Mount, as He talks about right ways and wrong ways to approach God; that is, *how to pray*. (It is also found in Luke 11.)

Today, besides being included in religious ceremonies around the world, this prayer is traditionally shared at the close of meetings we call "recovery groups." This specific use began in connection with Alcoholics Anonymous but today is often included in Twelve Step programs of personal development across a much wider spectrum.

Standing in a circle of held hands, those who pray the prayer are in fact, not just theory, calling on God as their Higher Power—taking the first step to merge their wills with God's will. This simple act, occurring around the world daily wherever people have "admitted they were powerless" and "come to the end of their own resources," is a powerful witness to the truth and wisdom of Jesus' words to His Father while He was on earth.

In *The Lord's Prayer: Peace and Self-Acceptance for Those in Recovery,* I have taken the phrases from the Lord's Prayer, line by line, and paired them with some of the Al-Anon slogans that especially relate to each section. These slogans are capsulized bits of wisdom about living that are shared and practiced, a day at a time, by recovering people in Al-Anon and other Twelve Step support groups.

The slogans may at first seem deceptively simple—even simplistic—when viewed apart from the framework of the Twelve Steps and the fellowship of recovery. But many of us have found that as we affirm and live the precepts, they can serve to illumine our individual situations, to help us cope, and then to go even deeper. As we meditate on such widely shared and proven wisdom, we can reach new levels of responsibility, understanding, and recovery.

Some of the most valuable things are found in small packages. As one slogan itself says, "Keep it simple." This simplicity, which has taken into account the truth and finds in it just the kernel that is sought, sometimes requires that we first go through confusion and complexity. Vernon Howard has written, "One sign of mental maturity is to comprehend the power and delight of simplicity."

The words of comfort and guidance found in the Lord's Prayer are for everyone—longtime believers and those new to faith and to the fellowship of recovery worldwide. They are as true and as effective today as they were in ancient times. Our slogans help us to relate the words of the prayer to modern life and its choices, to see the real issue in whatever we are currently struggling with.

It is my desire that each chapter of *The Lord's Prayer: Peace and Self-Acceptance for Those in Recovery* will offer a focus and a guide to living in the path of recovery and serenity, day by day. The chapters follow the wording of the individual phrases of the Lord's Prayer to allow a progression of understanding just who we are before our Father, as well as the gifts God wants to offer us. May the familiar words touch our hearts and our understanding as we look at them in this new way.

# CHAPTER 1

# *L*ET GO AND *L*ET GOD

*Our Father in heaven, Hallowed be Your name.*

ANYONE who wants to come to God must believe that there is a God and that he rewards those who sincerely look for him.

—Hebrews 11:6 TLB

ONCE a little girl was rehearsing a poem which she was to recite at a school festival. As soon as she found herself on the platform, the child looked anxiously round the schoolroom, her voice quivered, and shook with sobs. Then her father stepped from behind a partition where he had been watching the child, and took her in his arms, and asked her why she was troubled. And she answered, "Because I could not see you. Let me stand where I can look right into your face, and I shall not be afraid."

—H. J. Wilmot-Buxton,
*Prayer and Practice*

"WE admitted we were powerless and that our lives had become unmanageable." This is the all-important first step in any Twelve Step program, and as simple as it sounds, its words are a powerful key to serenity of spirit and a life that is truly worth living.

This chapter is about beginnings—and it is also about focusing on God the Father to whom Jesus prays in confidence and peace in the context of teaching His disciples.

Beginnings are important—they set the tone for all that follows. They open doors, turn on lights, let in fresh air, and sometimes position us in new directions.

I have one of those little plastic bank cards that looks like a credit card but actually only gives me access to the money in my checking account. The resources are there, ready to be set in motion by the electronic money-machine when I insert the card, give the right four-letter password, and press the correct buttons.

I admit that the speed and efficiency of this method have won me over, despite some anxiety that I couldn't "talk to" the machine if I made a mistake or if I had a question. I cross the threshold, electronically, every time I trust the system and insert my card. I relax and let it work for me. That first step gives me access to what is already mine.

The first of the Twelve Steps is also a threshold that admits us to resources that are actually ours already. We are entitled to live in serenity, and Christ calls us to that level of peace. Many have taken the first step and found that it leads only one direction: toward a wholeness that has been so elusive to us in the past—finally, a sense of being in the right place at the right time.

Some of us have tried other ways of coping: escape into work, pleasures, or overseeing the lives of people around us. Others may have fallen into destructive habits and become entrapped in addictions. Or some may be stuck in patterns of behavior that are self-defeating and seem unbreakable.

All of these things may look like a way of survival at the time. But any behavior turned to in desperation and extreme need—even in the guise of religious devotion—is not the answer. God Himself is the only One who can help us live life as we are meant to: in peace and serenity.

Jesus expressed this truth in Matthew 6 by illustrating the *right* way to pray with a focus on the priority of God and His kingdom: "Hallowed be Your name."

Where do we begin? We begin with the familiar name of God the Father, the One who has power in heaven and on earth to show us how to live, what to do next, and what choices to make.

Polly Berrien Berends writes in her book *Gently Lead: How to Teach Your Children About God While Finding Out for Yourself* of a mother who takes her son to the pastor of their church because she is very concerned that, as he has been memorizing the Lord's Prayer, he has learned the beginning all wrong. The minister takes her son into his study and asks him to say the prayer. "Our Father which art in New Haven, how do you know my name?" the child begins.

When the two emerge from the study, the mother asks with concern, "Well, did you straighten him out?" The pastor is quick to reply, "No, I wouldn't change a word of the way he says the Lord's Prayer. His way shows that he understands two important things about God: first, that God is very near; second, that God knows him personally."

We, too, are called to get the nugget of truth right. God is very near or we would not be addressing Him; and because He knows us personally, we may approach Him in prayer.

And as believers, we do "hallow" God's name. We acknowledge not only the nearness but the holiness of the One whom we implore. We heed these words: "Glory in his holy name; let the hearts of those who seek the LORD rejoice" (1 Chron. 16:10 NIV).

The opening words of the Lord's Prayer correspond to the first step in turning our lives over to God's power—letting go of our need to control ourselves and those around us. In the phrase "Our Father," we acknowledge that the answer lies beyond us—yet we *can* reach out and receive it.

We admit that trying to act as dictators in our own lives was a losing proposition, that we were no good at it, and that the ensuing guilt and frustration have finally sent us back to square one: the threshold of recovery, a fresh vision, and a new beginning.

What a wonderful place to be! Embarking on any journey, especially when it means turning ourselves around to head in an entirely different direction, is frightening, sometimes overwhelming. It takes great courage to admit what Scripture has said about our condition as human beings: that no one is truly righteous of himself or is ever able to save himself (see Rom. 3:23).

It is a staggering reminder that we can't get it right no matter how hard we try; but it is a blessed relief to admit that our recovery doesn't depend entirely on us and our efforts but is also related to the work and love of Someone Else—a Higher Power who has revealed Himself to us in Scripture, God the Father to whom Jesus prays this prayer.

Carroll E. Simcox writes in his book *Living the Creed*:

> God loves us and desires us, not because He needs us, but because it is His holy nature to love. He loves us not for His own sake or in the hope that He will enrich Himself by possessing us, but for our sake, for our good alone. God loves because He cannot help loving. . . . God loves us, not for what we can give Him or do for Him, but for what He can give us and do for us.

For the Christian on the path to recovery, the Higher Power is Christ, in God, through the power of the Holy Spirit. This line of power and authority is affirmed again and again in Scripture. Thus we can, like Christ, call upon the Father in confidence and peace. We know that it is God's nature to hear us and to be a very present help in our need, whatever it might be, however we might perceive it. As Paul wrote, "For it is God who works in you to will and to act according to his good purpose" (Phil. 2:13 NIV).

All that is needed in this approach is that we acknowledge our condition before God, affirm God's power to reach us, and begin to discover the first step in the way God has prepared to turn us back to Him and bring us home. This is the answer to a longing deep within us.

What do we mean by "home"? Some have called it "the journey" or "the way." In the language of recovery, home is serenity, acceptance, and the peace with God and neighbor that is possible when we surrender, take the first step, and stop trying so hard. "Let go and let God . . ." We will begin to understand some of the depth of the feeling of being at one with ourselves, with others, and with God as we step out in faith.

Home is also heaven, and in the words of one saint, "All the way to heaven is heaven," when we are on the way, choosing God and the life in Christ that is available to us each day, in each step. This means not only calling on God for ourselves but honoring God in the way we treat each person we encounter in our lives.

Vincent Ferrer writes, "If you truly want to help the soul of your neighbor, you should approach God first with all your heart." For us this is always the first step.

Simply saying these opening words of the Lord's Prayer shows that we acknowledge that "God is God; and we are not." God is "hallowed" or holy—perfect and to be honored above all living creatures. And even God's name—unpronounced by the Hebrews out of reverence—is to be approached in awe and sincerity.

Many people balk at this point, this threshold of recovery, because it seems to require admitting that we have failed in our lives up to this point. We haven't figured out how to live well. We haven't given it our best shot, or we have and it just hasn't worked out. Other people got in the way. We couldn't keep up our good intentions. We can rationalize endlessly about why the whole thing just wasn't working for us.

But at the threshold of turning to God, all our reasons and excuses fall away. We don't need them anymore. We need empty hands, ready to receive . . . a heart that is turned upward . . . a life that is willing to be opened up and filled by love.

Letting go is essential if God is to give us what we need and do what is best for us, to bring us to the place we should be this very moment. We gain strength and understanding from calling on God by name and admitting our helplessness next to God's holiness, might, and status as Lord.

We also need the practical side—the simple reminder that it is in these circumstances, whatever they may be, that God asks us to surrender. It is never too early or too late to take the first step, and we are the only ones who can do it for ourselves. In Al-Anon we acknowledge:

- I am not special. (I need this discipline, this truth, as much as anyone else.)
- And I am not helpless. (No one else can take this step for me; and I *can* do it.)

Being both special and helpless could serve as excuses to keep us out of recovery forever. What if no one really understands our particular situations? What if this approach just doesn't work for us?

Or maybe we're just too old, stupid, late, slow, nervous, preoccupied . . . whatever, to really catch on. If only we hadn't lost our friends, husbands, wives, teachers, pastors, we might be able to make it.

Stop! The following process is for us, and it is like a healing stream that can be stepped into at any point. Beginning also means dropping our excuses, trusting the process, and deciding to take the journey.

In subsequent chapters we will see other dimensions, new directions we are being led once we cross the threshold of acknowledging God, calling on God by name, and letting go and experiencing the divine power in our lives.

## PUTTING IT INTO PRACTICE

1. How are we accustomed to approaching God in our daily prayers? What new understanding do we now bring to that beginning?

2. What tasks in our life of recovery could we

begin today? How is God calling us to make a start or a fresh attempt in some area of life?

3. Psalm 44 provides a beautiful prayer for us in our consecration of our lives to the Father, our admission of our own weakness, and our hopes for future victories in the quest for serenity:

> O God, we have heard of the glorious miracles you did in the days of long ago. Our forefathers have told us. . . . They did not conquer by their own strength and skill, but by your mighty power and because you smiled upon them and favored them.
>
> You are my King and my God. Decree victories for your people. For it is only by your power and through your name that we [conquer]; I do not trust my weapons. They could never save me. Only you can give us the victory. . . . My constant boast is God. I can never thank you enough! (Ps. 44:1–8 TLB).

# CHAPTER 2

# FIRST THINGS FIRST

*Your kingdom come.*

*B*UT seek first his kingdom and his righteousness, and all these things will be given to you as well.

—Matthew 6:33 NIV

*I*T is important to recognize that it is useless to seek God somewhere else. If you cannot find Him here you will not find Him anywhere else. This is important because it is only at the moment that you recognize this that you can truly find the fullness of the Kingdom of God in all its richness within you; that God is present in every situation and every place, that you will be able to say, "So then I shall stay where I am."

—Metropolitan Anthony Bloom

*B*Y calling on God's name and asking for the help of our Higher Power, we are truly starting at the beginning. We have turned to God because focusing on ourselves and our troubles has gotten us nowhere. Oh, we may have been able to tie up a few loose ends, get some important work done, and even find a few things in our lives that look pretty good. But we know from past experience that without a real change in our perspective, "the center does not hold." Life is and has been unmanageable from where we stand. Perhaps that is because we have been looking in the wrong direction.

We will never find peace by overexamining our own lives, our own motives, our own situations. Instead, such gazing inward may make us feel simply further trapped by circumstances, murmuring, "If only . . ." If this is our problem, perhaps we need a widened perspective.

Harry Emerson Fosdick writes,

A person completely wrapped up in
himself makes a small package indeed.
The great day comes when a man begins
to get himself off his hands. He has lived,
let us say, in a mind like a room
surrounded by mirrors. Every way he
turned he saw himself.

Now, however, some of the mirrors change
to windows. He can see through them. He
begins to get out of himself—no longer the
prisoner of self-reflection but a free person
in a world where persons, causes, truths
and values exist, worthful for their own
sakes. Thus to pass from a mirror-mind to
a mind with windows is an essential
element in the development of a real
personality.

The way to find inner peace and the joy of
the kingdom of Christ within us is, paradoxically, to gaze outward.

The wisdom of the saints in this regard is always to stop, look, and listen. At this point in the journey of recovery, it is essential to turn your eyes toward Jesus and toward the peace He offers: "My peace I give to you; not as the world gives do I give to you. Let not your heart be troubled, neither let it be afraid" (John 14:27).

The peace that Jesus offered His disciples was not an escape from their difficult lives, which had become tied up with Him and His work in the world. It was not an excuse to retire into safety and seclusion away from the demands of ministry and struggle. Rather, it was a way of going on in courage within the very circumstances in which they found themselves: as cohorts of a rebel identified with insurrection and with disruption. Little did they know what was ahead of them—what victories and what dangers. Yet they knew who their Master was: Jesus Christ, the Son of the Father. And looking to Him was the key to finding the way to live.

Peace—serenity—is a gift that God grants to us in the inner person. It is a state of the individual heart that is receptive to God's Word and His work, in this moment, wherever it may lead. Somehow, through each of our individual choices to say "yes" to that peace, God is building a kingdom.

This prayer from the helpful guide *One Day at a Time in Al-Anon* expresses beautifully that sense of peace: "I will not let my inner peace be disturbed by the confusions around me. I will be gentle and tolerant, while maintaining my right to my individuality. I will listen and appreciate, and not judge the source of what I hear."

In this peace we are fully alive to both the moment and what it may bring, yet not bound to the limitations of what seems to be the situation. We present ourselves open to what God will do even here, even now.

The familiar phrase from the Lord's Prayer, "Your kingdom come," appears in this form in the synagogue Kaddish: "May he establish his kingdom during your life and during your days, and during the life of all the house of Israel." It is a prayer for peace and order within the individual life, and thus it is not surprising, though it stretches our understanding, to read that Christ says, "The kingdom of God is within you" (Luke 17:21).

John A. Sanford writes in his book *The Kingdom Within* of Jesus' parables of the hidden treasure and the pearl of great price:

> "The kingdom of heaven is like treasure hidden in a field which someone has found; he hides it again, goes off happy, sells everything he owns and buys the field" (Matt. 13:44). . . . "Again, the kingdom of heaven is like a merchant looking for fine pearls; when he finds one of great value he goes and sells everything he owns and buys it" (Matt. 13:45–46). . . .
>
> So the paradox is that the kingdom is both that which we find within ourselves as an inner treasure and also that which is searching to find us, *who when found become something of supreme value in the eyes of God. We* are the fine pearls if the kingdom can take root within us, and to us God gives a place of supreme value in his creation. (Italics added)

Thus this very familiar phrase, "Your kingdom come," bears much more weight than we could perhaps imagine. Yet it is also very simple, and praying it is a matter of choosing to align ourselves with God and God's purposes in the world—for ourselves and for all others.

We don't have to know what is next; we don't have to try to manage the other people in our lives; we don't have to decide ahead of time what choices we will make if this happens or that happens. We simply desire to put first things first. We turn around. We look up. We take a step closer to God's perspective by underlining or reaffirming the "yes" that we have already said to our Higher Power in the beginning.

The hardest time for me to say the "yes" that brings peace is in the early morning hours as I am waking. My dreamful sleep may have been quite healing and may have "knit up the ravell'd sleeve of care," as Shakespeare put it. Yet the first stroke of consciousness can bring unruly details to my mind: loose ends I feel I can't possibly manage to tie up; difficult problems that are yet (and perhaps perpetually) unsolved; too much work to be accomplished in sixteen waking hours; and no clear sense of priority.

"First things first" for me, then, has to be a reordering of my focus, not the accomplishing of one all-important, end-tying task. Sometimes this refocusing is best accomplished by simply praying the Serenity Prayer:

God grant me the serenity
    to accept the things I cannot change;
Courage to change the things I can;
    and wisdom to know the difference.

The Serenity Prayer is not just for the addicted person. It is for us all. This wonderful prayer tells us first that there are elements in our lives we have no power to change. Our serenity depends on accepting them. The more we try to fight them, the more they will torment us. Having the "courage to change the things I can" is realistic and allows me to work on those things that really are my concerns.

In Elizabeth Goudge's wonderful novel *The Scent of Water,* one of the characters, a kindly clergyman, offers a young girl three prayers that can help her reestablish her priority of "first things first." They are "Lord, have mercy," "Thee I adore," "and Into thy hands."

"Lord, have mercy." How often this prayer comes to mind in our helplessness. We acknowledge our dependence on God and the divine property always to have mercy toward us in our situation. And we find comfort in God's mercy.

"Thee I adore." This prayer turns our eyes once again upon our Lord in worship and adoration. It is the beginning of wisdom and understanding, in whatever condition we may utter it, for it expresses truth and positions us before the Almighty.

"Into thy hands." With these words we can commit any matter we are facing, now and for the future, into God's control. It will find a much better resting place there than anywhere else, and we will find our burdens lightened as we pray believing.

These three simple prayers, three words each, reflect the trinitarian nature of our God; thus they express our theology. But the most important thing about them is how they work. Each carefully worded phrase faces us toward Christ and His kingdom. And in each simple prayer, we are looking to God and not to ourselves for the answers.

It is a lesson we must learn and relearn. Peace and serenity are part of God's nature and transcend our individual lives. Yet we can know them in Christ and participate in His life by our free choice.

Prayer connects the two—God and us. It sets up a line of extension whereby, in the words of George Herbert's poem "Antiphon":

> The heavn's are not too high
> His praise may thither fly:
> The earth is not too low,
> His praises there may grow.

And so may God's kingdom grow, in our hearts, in our lives, along our way. "First things first" means that the long journey for us as individuals must begin with a single step—and we must make the choice to take it.

It is a step we repeat over and over again as

we enter the circumstances of each new day on earth that is granted us. We can never start in the middle. We are always beginners in the path of recovery *today*.

But the joy of that fact is the company we are allowed to keep. Christ is with us, nurturing His kingdom in us and in all willing others. And we have the comforting and challenging fellowship of other recovering persons as we struggle together on the way. We have the literature of recovery that is increasingly available to us to remind us of the important steps we can take right now, in each situation, to get us through this minute, this hour, this day. And we have God's assurance that somehow our consent, our opening ourselves up to the divine will, speeds the kingdom and its work in the world.

Today, we can choose to put "first things first" in our lives, and we can invite someone else to choose God's perspective and His kingdom. When we tell others how it works for us, we have turned from mirrors and opened small windows in the walls of our isolation for another to see through to find hope.

## PUTTING IT INTO PRACTICE

1. What are the "first things" staring me in the face today with which I must deal? How does prayer prepare me for my tasks today?

2. How have I seen God's kingdom coming in small ways in the past week, in the last year, or throughout my life to this point?

3. "Every moment is God's own good time, His kairos. The whole thing boils down to giving ourselves in prayer a chance to realize that we have what we seek. We don't have to rush after it. It was there all the time, and if we give it time, it will make itself known to us," wrote Thomas Merton.

Pray: Lord, show me what is already there; help me to accept it and give thanks. Show me also how to be open to Your kingdom coming in my own life and in the lives of others. Amen.

# CHAPTER 3

# *L*IVE
# AND
# *L*ET LIVE

*Your will be done*
*On earth as it is*
*in heaven.*

*T*EACH me to do your will,
  for you are my God;
may your good Spirit
  lead me on level ground.
                    —Psalm 143:10 NIV


*A* MAN'S life or death cometh from his neighbour; if we benefit our brother we benefit ourselves, and if we offend him we sin against God.
                    —*The Paradise of the Fathers*

*W*HEN we hold hands at the close of a recovery group meeting and say together the Lord's Prayer, one fact is tangible and clear: we are in this together or not at all. God's peace in us and God's kingdom within us have everything to do with our neighbors.

If God's will is our goal and choice, it necessarily involves the others in our lives and God's purposes for them. As someone has said, "Our neighbor's peace is at least half our own peace."

The apostle Paul writes to the Colossians, reminding them that true peace is attained in and through Christ: "For it pleased the Father that in Him all the fullness should dwell, and by Him to reconcile all things to Himself, by Him, whether things on earth or things in heaven, having made peace through the blood of His cross" (1:19–20). This means all people, those we perceive as friends, those we perceive as enemies, and those to whom we feel indifferent.

God's kingdom means the work of Christ in each person, the forgiveness for past misdeeds that is offered us when we confess, the hope of abundant life on the journey ahead, and the fellowship of others who also are willing to turn to God and discover the kingdom within.

Learning how to relate to the others we encounter is a lifetime process. But it begins here and now, and it is an important part of the letting go that we have begun to practice in our relationship with our Higher Power—with God the Father, in Christ, through the Holy Spirit.

This line from the Lord's Prayer, "Your will be done on earth as it is in heaven," teaches us something about the nature of God and His will. God is sovereign, in control, overseeing all. This truth is reflected in the following words attributed to the New Testament lawyer Gamaliel: "Do his will as thy will, that he may do thy will as his will."

What does it mean to do God's will? C. S. Lewis wrote in *The Great Divorce:* "There are only two kinds of people in the end: those who say to God, 'Thy will be done,' and those to whom God says in the end, '*Thy* will be done'"—even if the end result is complete separation from God. Yet he also adds, "No soul that seriously and constantly desires joy will ever miss it."

God will not force our hand. God desires that our own individual will be truly aligned with the divine purpose. Then we will see that this peace is for everyone and that we ourselves are called to be carriers and instruments of that peace.

When our focus is on God, on this kingdom coming for ourselves and others, our prayer and our hope will always be for unity with others in the process. Our old attitudes and even our former expertise in manipulating others—persuading them that we are right, coercing them to our side—will change. We will begin to see new possibilities of loving our neighbors in the light of this understanding and perspective. This is what it means to align our wills with God's will for the salvation of the whole world.

"Live and let live" means opening our hands, the hands that liked to pull strings and make other people nervously dance to our tune.

Or the hands that were greedy and tried to grasp all of the available treasure before anyone else could get any.

Or the hands that were folded and idle and were our excuse to sit back and let others take responsibility that we should have shouldered ourselves—or shared, at the very least.

Each of us knows in what way this speaks to our very situation.

In the Traditions of Al-Anon, the Fifth Tradition addresses this issue: "Each Al-Anon Family Group has but one purpose: to help families of alcoholics [substitute other recovering persons as applies]. We do this by practicing the Twelve Steps of AA *ourselves,* by encouraging and understanding our [addicted] relatives, and by welcoming and giving comfort to families of [addicted persons]."

We are a people for others. And the means of coming to the place of helping others is self-discipline: following the Twelve Steps, living by the slogans, and as Christians, integrating these principles into our understanding of Scripture and into our prayer life.

In order to have a sense of what it means for others to live in God's will and with God's peace, we must learn what it is to live, to know life more abundantly. The letting go serves us well at every step, especially here where we are essentially in the dark, experiencing a free-fall, and waking up to a new dimension of God's purposes for us.

I have learned that when I am asked to trust God in the dark and to suspend my need either to know or to control all of the outcomes of difficult situations in my life, much becomes possible.

First, I can relax because I've admitted that everything does not depend on me.

Second, I become much more aware of people around me and my stake in their lives and theirs in mine.

Third, I feel my situation widening out rather than closing in as I am suddenly receptive to new possibilities that were not on my list of either/or when I was doing it all myself.

What a relief! As the psalmist put it, "You have set my feet on level ground."

These steps of choosing "Your will be done" do not always come consciously or automatically. And I fight them constantly without even knowing it. Often it takes a verse of Scripture, a word of encouragement and perspective from a wise person, or an event in my life that makes everything suddenly appear in an entirely new light. Something happens to turn me around, back to facing Jesus, back to the fellowship of which I am a part even when I don't feel it.

In Ecclesiastes 4:10 we read: "If one falls, the other pulls him up, but if a man falls when he is alone, he's in trouble" (TLB).

God is the One who takes the blinders off our eyes, at various points along the journey, to remind us that we do not walk alone, we do not struggle singly. To "live" and to "let live" necessarily go together. When we are shouldering our own burden and responsibility in whatever we are currently facing, paradoxically, we are part of the peace of persons around us as well.

When we are living fully in the possibilities God offers to each of us, we are an encouragement, a sign of hope and of tangible help to one another. When we act with integrity along the way, we make space for others to follow suit, to fear less what they may have to lose, and to trust God's will for another day.

Most important to this prayer for God's will in our lives and in the lives of others is a belief in the inflatable quality of love. It's not a pie that has only so many pieces to go around and then there is no more. Rather, love expands, like the dough that Jesus in one place in Scripture likens to the kingdom of heaven: "The kingdom of heaven is like leaven, which a woman took and hid in three measures of meal till it was all leavened" (Matt. 13:33). There is enough to go around. God's will only annihilates our wills in order to absorb and include them in His purposes. And He does this in each heart that is willing to seek this way.

"Many will come from the east and the west, and will take their places at the feast with Abraham, Isaac and Jacob in the kingdom of heaven" (Matt. 8:11 NIV), we are told. We are invited to that feast, not because of anything special about us or the things we have done. It is free for the taking, open to the asking. And the invitations to others are unlimited.

"God's will" seems such an abstract concept. Even "God's kingdom" requires illustrations and examples to help us get at its truth. But the call to "live and let live" provides us with a very practical and tangible key to the kingdom.

Love for ourselves and the lives God has given us, and a desire to see others also live in love and in the fullness of peace—these are goals for which we can pray daily.

And thus we will see the kingdom grow— hand in hand, heart to heart.

## PUTTING IT INTO PRACTICE

1.  Dietrich Bonhoeffer wrote in *The Cost of Discipleship:*

> What is . . . love? Love which shows no
> special favour to those who love us in
> return? When we love those who love us,
> our brethren, our nation, our friends, yes,
> and even our own congregation, we are

no better than the heathen and the publicans. Such love is ordinary and natural, and not distinctively Christian.

We can love our kith and kin, our fellow countrymen and our friends, whether we are Christians or not, and there is no need for Jesus to teach us that. . . . He takes that kind of love for granted. . . .

How then do the disciples differ from the heathen? What does it really mean to be a Christian? Love that is extraordinary, unusual, which is not a matter of course. It is unreserved love for our enemies, for the unloving and the unloved, love for our religious, political and personal adversaries.

In every case it is the love which was fulfilled in the cross of Christ. It is the love of Jesus Christ himself, who went patiently and obediently to the cross—it is in fact the cross itself. The cross is the differential of the Christian religion, the power which enables the Christian to transcend the world and to win the victory.

What does love mean to me?

2. What other Scripture passages support the concept of learning to "live and let live"? How does this apply to God's promise to bless all peoples (see Gen. 12:3)?

3. Pray these words of Amy Carmichael:

Think through me, Thoughts of God,
    And let my own thoughts be
Lost like the sand-pools on the shore
    Of the eternal sea.
        Amen.

# CHAPTER 4

# KEEP IT SIMPLE

*Give us this day
our daily bread.*

THEREFORE I tell you, do not worry about your life, what you will eat or drink; or about your body, what you will wear. Is not life more important than food, and the body more important than clothes? Look at the birds of the air; they do not sow or reap or store away in barns, and yet your heavenly Father feeds them. Are you not much more valuable than they?

—Matthew 6:25–26 NIV

GOD as Father is Source of life. "It is he that hath made us and not we ourselves." We are easily beguiled into a fatuous forgetfulness of this by the very constancy of His giving; its regularity, its vital necessity. We naturally take for granted the things we are never without and cannot exist without. Our Lord teaches us to pray, "Give us this day our daily bread," in the hope surely that we shall exercise a little imagination while we pray. Daily bread represents the even more elementary conditions of life: oxygen, the continuing vital action of every organ of our bodies, above all and through all the mysterious flicker of what we call life.

—Carroll E. Simcox, *Living the Creed*

THE path of recovery will often send us back to basics. We will learn to pray for what we really need for the day, for God's provision in this hour, and for the serenity that is possible under these circumstances.

The psalmist helps us put our situation in perspective:

> LORD, my heart is not haughty,
> Nor my eyes lofty.
> Neither do I concern myself with great
>     matters,
> Nor with things too profound for me.
> Surely I have calmed and quieted my
>     soul,
> Like a child weaned with his mother;
> Like a weaned child is my soul within me
>     (Ps. 131:1-2).

Perhaps we have tried to reach for too much, to understand it all from the beginning, before we're willing to take a first step. It is natural to want to know what we're getting ourselves into.

But look at our natural journey on earth. We begin as infants, small and unprotected, helpless and dependent, even for our daily sustenance. Yet in this innocence is also a wholeness that is difficult to achieve again in our lifetimes.

Choices beset us; troubles come. As we grow, we become increasingly alienated from ourselves as God originally made us: dependent and yet loved for who we are, created in God's image.

Babies have no anxiety about their daily bread, the life-giving milk provided by their mothers. They may scream and demand and expect. But they are also immediately and naturally receptive when their needs are met by mother's breast or bottle. They know the simplicity of acceptance and the serenity of rest.

But life seems to become increasingly complex, and it takes more to bring us to a place of peace. A. Philip Parham writes in *Letting God*:

Most of us have witnessed a three year old

in the midst of a temper tantrum. Soothing and soft words fall on deaf ears. Shouting and screaming back at the child fail. . . . We also can behave like frightened and frustrated children. Life often gets to be too much to handle! We cry out in exasperation and fury, "Please, please, for God's sake, somebody come and take this decision out of my hands; it's too big for me!"

Once we are in the position of asking for help, anything can happen. And sometimes the word to bring our peace is as simple as Christ's stilling the storm: "Peace, be still!" We best hear that word in our familiar places. Parham continues, "For a child that place is usually a crib, a song, or comforting and strong arms. For us it may be our meeting, our sponsor, a treatment center, or the arms of Christ."

Perhaps, at different times, each of the above will give a simple answer to our desire for rest and for comfort in our situations.

Yet how often do we pray and plead and even demand our requests of God? We forget to go directly to our Source, to agree to be held until the storm passes and all is well again. Or perhaps it does pass, seemingly of its own accord; then when some of the strands of our lives naturally work themselves out, we forget that we didn't accomplish all these solutions ourselves. We forget to give God the glory for the small details as well as the major victories in life.

God calls us to rest like weaned babies, to have quieted souls within us, and to give thanks for our daily provision from a position of acceptance and peace. Jean Baptiste de la Salle has written:

> The more you abandon to God the care of all temporal things, the more He will take care to provide for all your wants; but if, on the contrary, you try to supply all your own needs, Providence will allow you to continue to do just that, and then it may very well happen that even necessities will be lacking, God thus reproving you for your want of faith and reliance in Him.

We are the only ones who know or can learn what "keep it simple" means in the context of our own lives. Have we been tempted to accumulate more wealth and possessions than we can ever possibly enjoy in a lifetime? Have we become entangled in doctrinal differences with other Christians on matters such as the arguments over the number of angels dancing on the head of a pin? Has our image been gradually replacing our true self in our work life, our home life, or our own minds?

Madeleine L'Engle writes in *The Irrational Season*, "The most difficult thing to let go is my *self*, that self which, coddled and cozened, becomes smaller as it becomes heavier. I don't understand how and why I come to *be* only as I lose myself, but I know from long experience that this is so."

We need to be pulled back to basics through this section of the Lord's Prayer, which reminds us that our needs truly are simple: "Give us this day our daily bread." It is a reasonable request. We need sustenance to continue the journey. And the bread, the simple fare we request, is for "us," not just "me."

If we have lost our taste for the simple nurturing that God has promised us on the way, we may have become haughty or proud or may be straining to know beyond what we can know for today. This will lead only to confusion and despair, setting us back and disquieting our souls.

In C. S. Lewis's delightful book in the Narnia series *The Last Battle* some skeptical dwarfs are brought into the marvel of Narnia, with open sky and fresh flowers, but they think that they are still in a dark, smelly hole of a stable. Expecting the worst, they can't see what is really there for them, much less partake of it.

When they are offered a feast of "pies and tongues and pigeons and trifles and ices," the dwarfs eat greedily but still think that they are consuming stable food, "a bit of an old turnip" and hay and raw cabbage leaf. The rich goblets of wine that they are offered in the kingdom they take for "dirty water out of a trough that a donkey's been at!"

When we forget to keep it simple, to take what is offered so generously from God's hand, and to give thanks, we miss the good of what is given, our daily bread and its very real pleasures. What we receive may be far and above what we originally asked for, but we should remember that it was God's to give in the first place and see it as a generous provision and bounty.

We begin by praying simply for what we actually need, not because we limit God but because He will teach us through the simple trust we express. It is God who enlarges our situation and gives us more than we could have imagined. He is able to do "exceedingly abundantly above all that we ask or think, according to the power that works in us" (Eph. 3:20).

What began with a simple letting go and allowing God into our situations by calling on the Father through Jesus Christ brings us further down the way into a trust that God is still with us. We find that we cannot map out the path before us or even expect God to do that for us ahead of time.

Like God's provision for the people of Israel in the Old Testament, the manna that lasted only one day and then became totally inedible, our daily bread is one answer at a time, one day at a time.

If we look at the three earlier petitions in the

Lord's Prayer, we see that the verbs were passive: "Hallowed *be* Your name"; "Your kingdom *come*"; "Your will *be done* . . ."

But the fourth petition is an active request: "*Give* us this day our daily bread." We are expected to ask—to participate in an involved, conscious way—in this very immediate transaction.

One commentator has written that the whole tone of this prayer suggests that this very simple requesting and granting of daily bread is a foreshadowing of our future share in the messianic banquet, the supper of the Lamb to which we are all invited in God's kingdom.

The daily bread could mean "bread of the coming day"; the present, material bread, when received thankfully, becomes a foretaste of the bread we are to break together someday— when God's purposes for us on earth are completed.

Alexander Schmemann writes in *For the Life of the World*:

[God said]: "Behold I have given you every herb bearing seed . . . and every tree, which is the fruit of a tree yielding seed; to you it shall be for meat. . . ." Man must eat in order to live; he must take the world into his body and transform it into himself, into flesh and blood. He is indeed that which he eats, and the whole world is presented as one all-embracing banquet table. . . .

This image of the banquet remains, throughout the whole Bible, the central image of life. It is the image of life at its creation, and also the image of life at its end and fulfillment: ". . . that you eat and drink at my table in my kingdom."

How can we "keep it simple" when the demands of our lives are tying us up in complications beyond our control? Everywhere we look we see problems: in families, in society, in the world. No wonder we are tempted to try too hard, to tackle things head-on. If only the solutions *were* simple.

I'm reminded of the little woven Chinese finger-traps the children bring home from school as prizes. When you stick your finger in and try to pull it out, the trap tightens and your efforts are fruitless. But if you relax your finger and push gently toward the center, the trap widens and you can easily remove your finger.

Sometimes the ways to uncomplicate our lives are the simplest and most sane moves we can make. But they may become clear to us only when we relax, get back to basics, turn to God with open hands, and expect our daily provision—to eat, to drink, and to take what is given for our lives in this moment.

## PUTTING IT INTO PRACTICE

1. How can I take three positive steps to un-complicate my life today? This week?

2. In what sense is the gospel itself simple? How is it also profound and life-changing for me?

3. Thomas à Kempis wrote in *The Imitation of Christ,* "If we were a little severe with ourselves at the beginning, we should afterwards be able to do all things with ease and delight."

Pray: Lord, help me today to balance diligence and simplicity, faith and action, in what You are calling me to accomplish. Thank You for Your provision for my life, one day at a time. Amen.

# CHAPTER 5

# BUT FOR THE GRACE OF GOD

*And forgive us
our debts,
As we forgive
our debtors.*

BLESSED are the merciful, for they will be shown mercy.

—Matthew 5:7 NIV

REAL, cleansing forgiveness is a forgetting—a real canceling out of the past. When a hurt is forgiven, it is as if it never happened; it is gone—forgotten as a dream—never to return.

—A. Philip Parham, *Letting God*

WHEN we are being led day by day by God's hand, it is at once a humbling and an exhilarating experience. Our idea of ourselves among others is bound to change, to be affected by the simple trust that is necessary for us to get anywhere at all in recovery.

When we admitted before God that we were powerless over the addictions and compulsions in our lives and that the pattern of our daily experience was truly unmanageable by ourselves, we had to let go of our pride, our perfectionism, and our illusion that we were in control of our lives.

G. Peter Fleck writes in his book *The Blessings of Imperfection:*

> While we may—yes, we must—strive for perfection, perfection is not attainable. It is the striving toward perfection that counts. Only the idea of something can be perfect. Its material expression . . . cannot be

perfect. The resolve to make one's peace and live with inevitable imperfection is a creative act.

As we look around us at the people in our lives, the growing fellowship of recovering persons of which we are now a part, as well as at others still outside it, we see the faces of other human beings, also imperfect, also struggling. Some are faces of those who have wronged us; others, we may have sinned against, consciously or unconsciously.

What we acknowledge at this point in the Lord's Prayer is our awareness that we, too, are sinners, that we have fallen short in various ways of God's intentions for us.

As *The Book of Common Prayer* puts it: "Most merciful God, we confess that we have sinned against you in thought, word and deed, by what we have done, and by what we have left undone. We have not loved you with our whole heart; we have not loved our neighbors as ourselves. We are truly sorry and we humbly repent."

When we admit this, we confess our shortcomings before God and in the presence of others. We ask, "For the sake of your Son Jesus Christ, have mercy on us and forgive us; that we may delight in your will, and walk in your ways, to the glory of your Name. Amen."

Such a confession wipes the slate clean and enables a new beginning. It puts us once again on an even par with others who can also ask God for forgiveness, regardless of the past.

Since God is gracious to forgive when anyone repents and turns to Him, Scripture is clear that we are expected to participate in God's graciousness by also forgiving those who have especially wronged us.

We are told, "Judge not, that you be not judged" (Matt. 7:1). And Christ taught in that same chapter that we are to tend to our own repentance and repair before God—to remove the huge beam from our own eye before we complain about the small speck in another's eye (see vv. 3–5). In the New International Version of the Bible, the relative sizes of the two objects are rendered "the speck of sawdust in your brother's eye" and the "plank in your own eye." Perhaps that is because we all know what our own deepest faults are, which are not readily apparent to others. And if we are not conscientiously dealing with those hidden sins, it is outrageous of us to set ourselves up as judges over the faults of another.

This does not mean that we should not be discerning—in the company we keep, in what we teach our children, in those we emulate in our behavior in the future. We must be as wise as serpents, Christ said, but as harmless as doves (see Matt. 10:16).

Yet this simple slogan, "But for the grace of God," can help us put into perspective the forgiveness that is required of us daily in our walk with others. By acknowledging that we are not good in ourselves and that even our present circumstances are a gift of God, we can learn to become more tolerant of others.

We may look at the situations of others and think we understand their failings. But none of us really knows what pressures they are under, what oppression they might be living with, or how clouded their vision may be, so that despair overshadows God's goodness.

St. Thomas Aquinas wrote, "To love any one

is nothing else than to wish that person good."
In recovery, we learn that most of our judging
of others comes through an inability to forgive
ourselves, perhaps even to love and to wish
ourselves good. Thus we are often hardest on
those who exemplify what we fear in our own
souls and who exhibit the vices we are least
able to conquer.

Accepting ourselves as created in God's
image, we learn to accept God's love for us—
not so that we can continue in our sins but so
that God's love can lead us into a better way.

The philosopher Pascal wrote, "We implore
the mercy of God, not that He may leave us at
peace in our vices, but that He may deliver us
from them." This, too, will then become our
prayer for others who are caught in traps of
their own making.

Making a "searching and fearless moral inventory of ourselves" (Step 4) and admitting
"to God, to ourselves and to another human
being the exact nature of our wrongs" (Step 5)
are the steps we are asked to take as an approach to forgiveness.

Next, we are to humbly ask God to remove

our shortcomings. This is our approach to the phrase, "And forgive us our debts."

And the largeness of heart that we experience when we are forgiven, the cleanness and refreshment of our spirits when we have honestly faced ourselves and turned to God to restore us, can only take us forward into new life.

I love the beautiful expression of what recovery sometimes feels like, echoed in these lines from George Herbert's poem "The Flower":

> How fresh, Oh Lord, how sweet
> and clean
> Are thy returns! ev'n as the flowers in
> spring . . .
> Grief melts away
> Like snow in May,
> As if there were no such cold thing.

The experience of confession and admission of sin can lead us to the sincere forgiveness of others, desiring that they, too, might know the joy of restoration and peace. King David prayed,

Create in me a clean heart, O God,
And renew a steadfast spirit within
   me. . . .
Then will I teach transgressors Your ways,
And sinners shall be converted to You (Ps.
   51:10, 13).


One contrite heart can have an effect on another; one person in recovery can have the
power to draw someone else into the circle of
forgiveness and restoration that is possible in
Jesus Christ. When we confess our faults and
learn to forgive ourselves, we come to look at
others differently. We see them in the light of
our own joy in the grace of God and desire for
them as well this precious gift of serenity that is
a mark of the kingdom.

Yet forgiveness is not ignoring sin; that would
be "cheap grace." We are still to remain discerning persons, not lost in a sea of sentimen-
tality or wishy-washy acceptance of anything
and everything that another imposes on us.
True forgiveness is not simply to look the other
way when we are wronged.

Sometimes we must fully face the wrong

that has been done to us, name it for what it is, and live in the reality of painful awareness. This means we have to grow out of what psychologists call denial. Only by facing the truth squarely can we ever find healing of the wrongs that were done to us.

But simply acknowledging the reality of having been abused does not in itself bring healing. When we know what we are dealing with, we can begin to pray for forgiveness of persons who committed those very sins against us.

We will ask in faith that the past may be mended in the new pattern of our lives in recovery—through cooperation with God's forgiveness in Christ.

Those of us who are related to addicted people must always be wary of abuse, not only of others but of ourselves. We never do the abuser a favor by giving that person the benefit of the doubt when we have truly been wronged. Rather, we enable him to continue in his addiction and abuse if we do not stand up for the truth and refuse to allow anyone—even ourselves—to suffer needlessly. Though we may continue to love a person who has wronged us, there are times when we must remove ourselves physically from such a one to avoid further, ongoing abuse.

Aelred of Rievaulx in his classic work *Spiritual Friendship* writes of the conditions by which, according to Scripture, friendship is "wounded and dissolved; namely, insults, reproaches, betrayal of secrets, pride, and the stroke of treachery." We must be discerning in protecting ourselves as well as others from the trap of continuing sin.

We can extend and receive forgiveness tangibly and change the nature of our relationships only when we are dealing with a sane and honest "other" who is also able and willing to give and to receive. Sadly, a true exchange of confession and forgiveness is not always possible with the person closest to us or the one with whom we most need restoration. So we sometimes must live with this sadness.

Yet even when actual restoration is not feasible, we know that we are called to exercise compassion, a steady stream of forgiveness and concern, that operates through us as though God's purposes were already accomplished—

as though the kingdom had already come and the unity we long for in Christ were already a reality.

"But for the grace of God" reminds us that all is grace. We can proceed on the way only as we are willing to forgive, whether our relationships can be restructured and reforged or not. We act in faith in cooperation with God's desire for all to find forgiveness. That, too, is our hope.

"For now we see in a mirror, dimly," Paul wrote in his first epistle to the Corinthians, "but then face to face. Now I know in part, but then I shall know just as I also am known" (1 Cor. 13:12).

In our current situation of limited sight, forgiveness is the only way in which to walk, day by day, by God's grace.

## PUTTING IT INTO PRACTICE

1. Arthur Gordon writes in his book *A Touch of Wonder* about Jesus' parable of the good Samaritan: "Where does it come from—this capacity to share another's grief or feel another's

pain?" When he asked this question of a wise old minister, the answer came: "Empathy, courage, the habit of helping."

How can we practice one or all of these traits in our circumstances today?

2. How has the forgiveness of others toward you made a difference in your life? What about the effects of your forgiveness of those who have wronged you?

Pray: Lord, may Your compassion fill my heart today as I see others in the light of Your loving forgiveness. Amen.

# CHAPTER 6

# *L*ISTEN AND *L*EARN

*And do not
lead us into
temptation,
But deliver us
from the evil
one.*

*B*E careful—watch out for attacks from Satan, your great enemy. He prowls around like a hungry, roaring lion, looking for some victim to tear apart. Stand firm when he attacks. Trust the Lord; and remember that other Christians all around the world are going through these sufferings too.

—1 Peter 5:8–9 TLB

*T*HERE is no worse enemy of the soul than you yourself, if you are not in harmony with the Spirit.

—Thomas à Kempis,
*The Imitation of Christ*

*A* RECENT children's animated film to which I took my five-year-old daughter portrayed a chilling example of evil. The villainous sea-witch did something even worse than killing her victims. She drained the life out of them until they became limp, colorless shadows of their former selves; and she kept them under her thumb, in servile captivity to her will.

This was the threat of control she held over other sea-creatures who wouldn't cooperate with her evil purpose, to usurp the authority of that domain and become queen of the ocean. Needless to say, her day of reckoning finally came. All of the captives were set free, and her evil reign was ended.

It was an exquisite and accurate picture of the inflated self and its effect on others, and although it scared my daughter, it also probably taught her more of sin and evil than any words alone could have done.

As adults, most of us have already encountered the reality of evil, sometimes very close to us or in the oppression of those dear to us. It is reasonable on our journey of recovery to pray, as some of the newer translations of the Lord's Prayer put it, "Save us from the time of trial, and deliver us from evil."

Even Christ, the night He was to be betrayed in the Garden of Gethsemane, told His disciples: "Pray that you may not enter into temptation" (Luke 22:40). Then He Himself prayed that the cup of suffering and death might be removed from Him if it were the Father's will. Nevertheless, He submitted to the reality of the cross when His time came.

It is a fearful world in which we cannot avoid the consequences of sin in all of society and in ourselves. Yet it is a world in which God has not forsaken us. We must be wise and wary; we must "listen and learn" from all of our experiences so that we can live in peace, as much as is possible, with ourselves and with others.

One commentator on the Lord's Prayer says, "Whether evil comes from other men, inner impulse, circumstances, or the enemy . . . prayer for deliverance is appropriate, and we may ask to be spared the final, overwhelming test." It is all right—in fact, it is necessary—to admit that we are human and that we find it difficult to stand against the evil opposing us.

Often part of our recovery means taking a stand against evil, standing up to and opposing abuse and manipulation, which are so often the destructive results of addictive patterns of behavior.

It is hard to see and know the truth, and it takes courage to act on what we do see—to stand up for what is right no matter what it may cost us.

But once again, we acknowledge that we are not alone. Someone has said, "Courage is simply fear that has said its prayers." No matter what level of extremity we are facing, if we have turned to God, face toward Jesus, there will be a strength and an awareness that God will "fight against those who fight against [us]" (Ps. 35:1).

It is hard to deny the existence of evil in our society today; and the kind of "innocence" that is a denial of the power of evil is no protection in the "time of trial." Rather, it is important for us neither to deny the reality of evil nor to be overly interested in its mentality and its workings. To study its methods too closely—except for those few people especially called to do battle on the front of the enemy—puts us in jeopardy.

We are wise to be wary, too, of the subtle temptations the devil may present to us. Dorothy L. Sayers has written that we must be able to recognize and resist Satan's "diabolic set-up." This "set-up" or "good side" that the devil shows to the world may seem to offer a noble, reasonable course of action for us to follow. But, she writes, "the nobler, the more dangerous. The Devil is a spiritual lunatic, but, like many lunatics, he is extremely plausible and cunning. . . . It is when the Devil looks most noble and reasonable that he is most dangerous."

In recovery, we are called upon to make fine distinctions, to determine not just what is expedient but what is God's will for us: "Do not conform any longer to the pattern of this world, but be transformed by the renewing of your mind. Then you will be able to test and approve what God's will is—his good, pleasing and perfect will" (Rom. 12:2 NIV).

We are often required, also, in our relationships with others to seek to distinguish between the sin and the sinner. We sometimes must acknowledge a difference between the addiction itself and the flawed, human, addicted person who is trapped in a destructive way of life.

In Al-Anon, people in close relationships with addicted persons are neither urged to leave the scene immediately nor encouraged to stay and endure to the bitter end. There is respect for the fact that each case is different. Likewise, every person in his or her walk with God is called upon to "listen and learn" how to live in a mode of healthy recovery and serenity, despite—and even because of—the outward circumstances.

These words express a prayer and a hope for the recovering person: "Whatever faces me at this time, I know that God has given me the power to set my world in order." We can always do something; we can take the next step—even if that step is prayer and waiting.

Often, we must act with courage in the moment and stand up to those who would trample on others, drain the life out of the helpless, or set an evil act into play in our world. We are here for a purpose, and our actions for good really matter. When we have prayed about a situation and accurately assessed it, our presence in love and compassion can even mean life or death to another person.

As part of recovery, each of us must listen and learn what God is teaching through the circumstances. Often, no one else can walk in our shoes enough to tell us what to do or what is truly required of us in a moral crisis.

In this sense, recovery means growing into responsible adulthood—not total self-sufficiency, for we always need one another. It also means a sense of shaping and developing our own lives with integrity, regardless of what may appear in the path as stumbling blocks or stepping-stones.

Part of listening and learning is to create some space in which God can act. Find some silence. Detach in a healthy way from the problem so that in a clear focus, some new solutions may present themselves. "When I detach my mind from what is troubling me, my problems often solve themselves. Or it may be that leaving them to God gives Him a chance to take a hand in my affairs," we read in *One Day at a Time in Al-Anon*.

Watching and waiting are elements of the abundant life that Christ desires for us. Victorious living can never come all at once in one magnificent sweeping act. Rather, the only way of recovery is one choice at a time—one moment, one day spent turned in the right direction, making whatever progress is possible with God's help.

We are right to fear evil; we are wise to recognize the threat of abuse and manipulation by others who would set themselves up as little gods and fool the unwary into meek submission.

Keeping our own perspective as teachable people before God is essential as we keep our eyes and ears open on the journey of recovery. Thomas Merton wrote, "All true prayer somehow confesses our absolute dependence on God. It is a vital contact with Him. It is when we pray truly that we really *are*. From our prayers we receive light to apply to our own problems and difficulties."

Look, listen, think, read, pray.
"Save us from the time of trial."
"Deliver us from the evil one."

The spirit and the actual deliverance of these prayers may be answered for us in ways we cannot yet envision.

## PUTTING IT INTO PRACTICE

1. Write down five things about your experiences today that might have gotten by you if you were not consciously "listening" and "learning."

2. Do you have a daily quiet time in which to "listen and learn" from God's Word?

3. "Never be completely unoccupied, but read or write or pray or meditate or do something for the common good," said Thomas à Kempis.

Pray: Lord, what would You have me hear, see, and do today for Your kingdom?

# CHAPTER 7

# ONE DAY AT A TIME

*For Yours is the kingdom and the power and the glory forever.*

$\mathcal{H}$E will always give you all you need from day to day if you will make the Kingdom of God your primary concern. So don't be afraid, little flock. For it gives your Father great happiness to give you the Kingdom.

—Luke 12:31–32 TLB

$\mathcal{T}$O see a world in a grain of sand
And a Heaven in a wild flower
Hold Infinity in the palm of your hand
And Eternity in an hour.

—William Blake

*T*HIS portion of the Lord's Prayer, known as the doxology, is a liturgical expression of the glory of God whom we address. It brings us back full circle to the very first phrase of the prayer, "Hallowed be Your name."

We have turned to God the Father in our need, in our desire to receive help for the unmanageable nature of a life that is out of relation with our Higher Power.

In this final phrase of the prayer, we recap the nature of God and all that is in God's hands. Thus we place ourselves, "one day at a time," in God's care while at the same time we choose both to live in and to further the kingdom by our choices, by our understanding, and especially by our treatment of others.

"For Yours is the kingdom and the power and the glory" is an expression of worship, a response to who God is—the One we have addressed and the One to whom we have prayed for guidance. The affirmation of our confidence in God's power and majesty adds light to all that has gone before and increases our hope for the future.

Commentator C. W. F. Smith writes,

> While fulfilment must await the last day, the kingdom, power, and glory are already in God's hands. We may pray for God's kingdom because the kingdom is his; for the hallowing of his name, because the glory is his; for the doing of his will because the power is his. We may share in the provision of bread, forgiveness, and deliverance also, because these are gifts that come with his kingdom; they express his power and manifest his glory.

This reminder of God's power and glory should give us a glimpse not only into the present reality of God with us but into what the future may bring as God's kingdom comes to fruition and completion. And the blessed part of this vision is that even now, *in this moment,* God is very near to us in all the details of our lives: the grace of health, the closeness of loved ones, the accomplishment of our work, and the enjoyment of all that is available to us each day.

God's purposes continue to be revealed in individual lives that are given over to God's will. As Christians, we believe that life is essentially a comedy. That doesn't mean that life lacks seriousness. Rather, in the classical sense, it means that we expect a happy ending.

We know that while we are on the journey, we are faced with trials, struggles, and absurdities beyond imagination. Yet in one sense, the victory is already assured. The skirmishes that are part of the larger battle might make things look bleak. But somehow all of these things are to be folded up into God's purposes for all of us and for the whole creation.

In his novel *Godric,* Frederick Buechner wrote a fictional narrative about the historical Anglo-Saxon monk of that name, based on the few available details of his life. Buechner portrays him as a very human, struggling saint, one who had in the past used others shamelessly, seeking only his own pleasure and personal gain.

After Godric spent half a life in turmoil and "trackless wastes," his life took an abrupt turn. God touched him; a heart "took root" and began to grow in him. Eventually he sold all his goods, left his home, and began the life of a hermit at Finchale, on the River Wear near Durham, England.

In a moment of vision, looking back on the path that got him to that place, he reflects, "What's lost is nothing to what's found, and all the death that ever was, set next to life, would scarcely fill a cup."

These are moments of epiphany, when for a brief split second we may see how God's kingdom has been growing within us, how God's power has gotten us to this very point of our lives, and how His glory touches us and the very spot of creation in which we make our home.

We, too, can catch a glimpse of the world in a grain of sand, heaven in the glory of a flower, and eternity in even a short time with a loved one.

In the New Testament, the kingdom of God is variously compared to a woman with a lost coin, a treasure in a field, a pearl that is greatly desired, sheep and a shepherd, a banquet or wedding feast, a vineyard, a mustard shrub that grows from the smallest of seeds, a lump of leaven. Each image gives us a small picture of the very tangible nature of growth or value in the process of becoming.

When we are tempted to bemoan the fact that we seem to be making such slow progress or even sliding back into prerecovery behavior, we would do well to look again at the slowness of the natural processes of life. It takes about nine months for a child to come to full gestation. Seeds lie buried underground in apparent death until the first sprouting of spring. Suddenly touched by God, people whose hearts seemed to be cold and hardened beyond change can emerge from their despair to join the living and begin their own journey among us.

In each of these cases, God's power and God's glory are part and parcel of the process. We may not see the workings of the Spirit in our lives or the lives of others, just as we do not see the roots growing underground. But when the plant breaks ground, we rejoice in the One who accomplishes all things in the proper time.

"One day at a time" is the only way to live, for saints and for ordinary people (which saints always were in the first place). We affirm the truths about God's kingdom, God's power, and God's glory not because we can see and feel their reality in every moment but because these truths transcend us and bring us up into their life and reality only as we surrender each moment to God.

We begin each day (or find time within a busy day) to redirect our thoughts toward God, our Higher Power. God is there, in power and glory, underlying and overshadowing the events of our day.

Prayer is not something we leave behind in our rooms; it is instead the vertical connection with God that exists even when we are not consciously practicing it. It corresponds to our deepest desires before God and an acknowledgment that God is very near and faithful to answer in the way that will prove best for us.

An unknown author has written:

I prayed for strength that I might
 achieve;
I was made weak that I might obey.
I prayed for health that I might do great
 things;
I was given infirmity that I might do
 better things.
I prayed for riches that I might be
 happy;
I was given poverty that I might be
 wise.
I prayed for power that I might have the
 praise of others;
I was given weakness that I might feel
 the need of God.
I prayed for all things that I might enjoy
 life;
I was given life that I might enjoy all
 things.
I received nothing that I asked for—all
 that I hoped for;
My prayers were answered—I am most
 blessed.

When we reach for unrealistic goals, think

that we can skip important steps in our recovery, or forget to affirm daily our relationship with God and all that it implies, it is easy to slip backward into despair.

But all of the tools of recovery as mirrored in the Lord's Prayer, the "summary of the Gospel," are available to us. And we have the whole wisdom of Scripture and many other books and helps available to us as we read, think, study, and pray, day by day.

Next time you attend a Twelve Step recovery group meeting, pray the Lord's Prayer silently before you enter the room. Let the assurances in the prayer underlie your experience of sharing with other people the many and various steps and facets of recovery.

Then, as you pray the prayer together at the closing, give thanks for all that has gone before and all that is yet possible because God's kingdom is being built in hearts, right there in that room and around the world.

Richard of Chichester declared,

Day by day.
Day by day.

O dear Lord
three things I pray:
To see thee more clearly
Love thee more dearly
Follow thee more nearly,
Day by day.

## *PUTTING IT INTO PRACTICE*

1. Mark on your calendar for the week one word for each day that expresses a quality you wish to exemplify in your life, such as *trust, joy, encouragement, peace,* etc.

2. The next week, choose one Bible verse a day to fit each of those characteristics. Based on the Bible's criteria, what have you learned about these attributes from trying to live them day by day?

3. "And whatever things you ask in prayer, believing, you will receive" (Matt. 21:22).

Pray: Lord, may I be open to the workings of Your kingdom, within and without my life, day by day.

# CHAPTER 8

# KEEP AN OPEN MIND

*Amen.*

$\mathcal{E}$VERYTHING is possible for [one] who believes.

—Mark 9:23 NIV

$\mathcal{L}$ORD
I'm at the end
Of all my resources.

*Child*
*You're just at the beginning*
*of Mine.*

—Ruth Harms Calkin,
*Lord, I Keep Running Back to You*

To pray, as we do at the end of the Lord's Prayer, "Amen," is to (*a*) solemnly ratify and (*b*) conclude, say the final word to all that has gone before. Our "Amen" underlines the truth of the prayer. Leaving it off is like leaving the period off the bottom of the exclamation point!

For the word really means to us a solemn "yes" to God's promises. The *New Jerome Biblical Commentary* points out that Jesus' use of "Amen" indicates His "teaching with authority as if he had the right to speak for God (without any indication that the word of God had come to him—he seemed already to possess it), and his assumption that what he said and did (by way of healing, etc.) was bringing the rule or kingdom of God into this world."

And *Peake's Commentary on the Bible* points out that "The Amen" is actually a proper name for Christ. Truly He is the beginning and end of our prayer; He is the One we seek and the means of our beginning to pray at all.

In our phrase-by-phrase discovery of ways in which Christ envisioned the coming of the kingdom in individual lives and the ways in which we are personally called to participate in that coming, we see how fitting this closure to the Lord's Prayer is.

"Amen" brings to a close our study of the Lord's Prayer, just as it signals the end of our meeting, the unclasping of hands, and the departure from one another's presence to take up our separate lives.

But having prayed and learned together, we are not exactly the same people we were when we walked in the door an hour or so before. As we leave we take with us something of the experience, whether we are consciously aware of just what it is or not.

"Amen" is a breaking point, a ratification, an endorsement, and a conclusion. But it can also be to us a sign that more lies ahead. If all of the above is possible, even *promised*—all of the petitions that we have prayed together—then *any-*

*thing* is possible. We can go on with our lives in confidence and peace.

Poet Ruth Harms Calkin writes graphically and delightfully of this truth in her poem "Enough Grace":

> Lord of my trembling heart . . .
> If there is enough ocean
> To keep one small fish swimming
> Then surely there is enough grace
> To keep one weak child standing.

We are to live in such trust, to keep an open mind and a heart that God has touched, so that all the experiences and people we encounter in the coming week are seen in the light of God's love and His purposes for us. Then surely this bountiful grace, experienced in the moment as we require it, will be enough to keep each of us "swimming" in the world to which we belong.

Having an open mind means that although we may end one day, one event, or one encounter with another person, whether the experience was good or bad, we have not yet seen all that God will do.

With each new day of recovery, we have only begun. One prayer we use in Al-Anon is: "I will make this day a happy one, for I alone can determine what kind of a day it will be."

"Keep an open mind" also means: "I pray to be relieved of the compulsion to worry about the past or to let my pessimism paint black pictures of what may happen tomorrow. I will keep in mind that we can live only in the present and that all the rest of life is either past or uncertain" *(One Day at a Time in Al-Anon)*.

And it means: "When I'm trying too hard to change things, when I forget to let go—when I demand too much, too soon, of myself and others, I'll ask God to remind me that Easy Does It."

Keep an open mind.
Let go and let God.
Put first things first.
Live and let live.
Keep it simple.
Remember, but for the grace of God . . .

Listen and learn.
Take one day at a time.
Easy does it.

Allow the open mind you are acquiring to bring these thoughts to you daily as they are appropriate: in the midst of turmoil, in your reading and praying, and as they serve as counterpoints to the truths of Scripture.

Ruth Calkin writes in "The Time Is Now":

Lord
I see with startling clarity
That life is never long enough
To put You off
Until tomorrow . . .
If I intend to walk with You tomorrow
I must start today.

Amen.

## THE LORD'S PRAYER

As our Savior Christ has taught us, we now pray,

Our Father in heaven
　hallowed be your name,
　your kingdom come,
　your will be done,
　　on earth as in heaven.

Give us today our daily bread.

Forgive us our sins
　as we forgive those
　who sin against us.

Save us from the time of trial,
　and deliver us from evil.

For the kingdom, the power
　and the glory are yours,
　now and for ever. Amen.

　—From *The Book of Common Prayer,*
　　　　　Eucharistic Rite II

## PRAYERS FOR RECOVERY

### Serenity Prayer

God grant me the serenity
To accept the things I cannot change,

Courage to change the things I can,
And wisdom to know the difference.

God help me to avoid the temptation to deceive myself by justifying my actions when they were wrong. Make me strong enough to do what I should to keep me serene. Amen.
—*One Day at a Time in Al-Anon*

## PUTTING IT INTO PRACTICE

1. What has God done in your life recently to which the best response is "Amen"?

2. How can you begin to share what you have learned about prayer with those closest to you? About trust? About serenity?

3. Here is a message to our hearts:

### You Are Free

O God
I read today

That the sons of Jacob
And their descendants
Had lived in Egypt 430 years.
But on the last day
Of the 430th year
Your people left Egypt
And the cruel bondage
They had painfully endured.
*This was the time You selected.*
God, what time have You selected
To free me from the cruel tyranny
That binds me without mercy to myself?

*Chosen child—*
*In My Son*
*You are even now*
*Completely free.*
*Accept your freedom!*
*Walk out this very moment*
*Into the radiant company*
*Of My people.*

—Ruth Harms Calkin,
*Lord, You Love to Say Yes*

Pray: Heavenly Father, help me to walk in Your freedom from this day forward. Amen.

# Sources

Jill Haak Adels, *The Wisdom of the Saints* (New York: Oxford University Press, 1987).

Isabel Anders, *Awaiting the Child: An Advent Journal* (Cambridge, Mass: Cowley Publications, 1987).

Aelred of Rievaulx, *Spiritual Friendship* (Kalamazoo: Cistercian Publications, 1977).

Polly Berrien Berends, *Gently Lead: How to Teach Your Children About God While Finding Out for Yourself* (New York: HarperCollins, 1991).

Dietrich Bonhoeffer, *The Cost of Discipleship* (New York: Macmillan, 1959).

Frederick Buechner, *Godric* (New York: Atheneum, 1981).

H. J. Wilmot-Buxton, *Prayer and Practice* (London: Skeffington & Son, 1894).

Ruth Harms Calkin, *Lord, You Love to Say Yes* (Wheaton, Ill.: Tyndale House, 1982).

Ruth Harms Calkin, *Lord, It Keeps Happening . . . and Happening* (Wheaton, Ill.: Tyndale House, 1984).

Amy Carmichael, *His Thoughts Said . . . His Father Said . . .* (Fort Washington, Penn.: Christian Literature Crusade, 1941).

G. Peter Fleck, *The Blessings of Imperfection: Reflections on the Mystery of Everyday Life* (Boston: Beacon Press, 1987).

Arthur Gordon, *A Touch of Wonder* (Old Tappan, N.J.: Fleming H. Revell, 1974).

Elizabeth Goudge, *The Scent of Water* (New York: Coward-McGann, 1963).

Madeleine L'Engle, *The Irrational Season* (New York: Seabury Press, 1977).

C. S. Lewis, *A Mind Awake,* edited by Clyde S. Kilby (London: Geoffrey Bles, 1968).

*One Day at a Time in Al-Anon* (New York: Al-Anon Family Group Headquarters, 1968, 1972, 1973).

H. Philip Parham, *Letting God: Christian Meditations for Recovering Persons* (San Francisco: Harper & Row, 1987).

David Rioux, *Twelve Months of Days* (Minneapolis: CompCare Publishers, 1990).

John A. Sanford, *The Kingdom Within: The Inner Meaning of Jesus' Sayings* (San Francisco: Harper & Row, 1987).

Dorothy L. Sayers, *A Matter of Eternity* (Grand Rapids: William B. Eerdmans, 1973).

Alexander Schmemann, *For the Life of the World* (St. Vladimir's Seminary Press, 1973).

Carroll E. Simcox, *Living the Creed* (New York: Morehouse-Gorham, 1954).

Charles Williams, *The New Christian Year* (London: Oxford University Press, 1941).

# The Twelve Steps
# of Alcoholics Anonymous

1. We admitted we were powerless over alcohol—that our lives had become unmanageable.

2. Came to believe that a Power greater than ourselves could restore us to sanity.

3. Made a decision to turn our will and our lives over to the care of God as we understood Him.

4. Made a searching and fearless moral inventory of ourselves.

5. Admitted to God, to ourselves, and to another human being the exact nature of our wrongs.

6. Were entirely ready to have God remove all these defects of character.

7. Humbly asked Him to remove our shortcomings.

8. Made a list of all persons we had harmed, and became willing to make amends to them all.

9. Made direct amends to such people wherever possible, except when to do so would injure them or others.

10. Continued to take personal inventory and when we were wrong promptly admitted it.

11. Sought through prayer and meditation to improve our conscious contact with God as we understood Him, praying only for knowledge of His will for us and the power to carry that out.

12. Having had a spiritual awakening as the result of these steps, we tried to carry this message to alcoholics, and to practice these principles in all our affairs.